"SEE ME"

The Invisible Autistic Boy

Written and Illustrated by
David Petrovic

Edited and Prefaced by
Sandy Petrovic

A true tale about kindness, worthiness, and the power to make a difference.

D1522245

www.petro-autism.com

Published September 2022 by
David Petrovic and Sandy Petrovic
ISBN: 9798841652328 (paperback)

www.petro-autism.com

This book is dedicated:

to ALL children who feel alone, unworthy, or unseen
And to Nick, who changed everything for me

Jacob,

Embrace a difference...
and MAKE a difference!

Special thanks to:

Frank Petrovic: for his idea to write a children's book, along with his brainstorming, love, and support

Erin Yilmaz: for her formatting, invaluable publishing assistance, amazing expertise, tireless support, and valued friendship (www.linkedin.com/in/erin-yilmaz)

Beth Anne Martin, Ph.D: for her consultation

Eeha Bhatt: cover art and the coloring sketch in "Part 3: Activities"
https://eehabh.wixsite.com/komorebi/
https://www.Instagram.com/Eeha_illustration/

Benjamin Michael Hall: back cover author headshot
https://benjaminmichaelphotography.pixieset.com

PREFACE for Parents and Teachers

I have known David Petrovic since before he was born, for I am his mother! I began noticing developmental differences in him by 15 months of age, and we learned that he was autistic early on as he progressed.

David received years of therapy and support to discover what he needed (and still needs) to manage his challenges and thrive. His amazing strengths, attitude, and spirit have allowed him to self-advocate and more than fulfill his potential. A recipient of special education through his elementary school years, David is now a middle school teacher with a master's degree in theology. Though virtually nonverbal until the age of three, David is now a national speaker and published author. And most importantly, David is comfortable with who he is. He is happy, and he is proud to be autistic.

Our mission is to teach others about autism and differences. In so doing, we wish to dispel stereotypes and promote the worth and abilities of every human being. Bullied as a tween and teen, David especially strives to eradicate this behavior. He encourages children to live with kindness and compassion by enlightening them on the effects of bullying and the power they have to make a difference for others. Having lived through feelings of unworthiness and seeing no purpose in his life, David strives to teach children the lessons he has learned to change that thinking.

As a mom, my ultimate pain lay in witnessing David's isolation and rejection by peers. His metamorphosis as he accepted his differences and discovered his worth was truly amazing and joyful to witness. Hence the origins of this book, particularly "Part 1."

While "See ME" may inspire children who have experienced challenges or special needs, it is intended for ALL children to encourage compassion and teach valuable lessons.

Following their read, enhance your children's learning:

"Part 2" presents a more detailed description of David's autism. In this format, we provide a deeper explanation of autism without distracting from the story itself. David relays the information in the same story voice, and children will experience autism from the inside out via the words of someone who lives it. So really, this book contains two stories in one, both with the goal of enlightening children in an interesting way.

And finally, realizing that experiential learning is most impactful and lasting, David and I have added a supplement of various activities to conclude the book. Throughout the tale, you will notice italicized words that may be new to your child. We hope that their meanings are discernible through context clues. Even if already known, the emphasis on these important words is warranted in today's society! They will show up again in the word search and crossword puzzles in "Part 3." These two activities enjoyed by young readers can further clarify and reinforce this vocabulary.

Reflecting on their own strengths and differences is also important for children's self-image and acceptance. I especially love the last posed question of why the "E" is backwards in the title. David's answer follows that page, but we appreciate and hope that other interpretations will emerge! This backwards E mimics the title of our previous book, which is described below.

It is our hope that the included activities will give opportunities for participation and discussion between parents/caregivers/teachers and the kids, or while older children or adults read this book to little ones (like book club reflections and discussion points, but for kids!).

Adults and teens may further enjoy our two-time award-winning: *Expect a Miracle: Understanding and Living with Autism* (**Revised 2nd Edition**). Written from each of our perspectives, this book enables readers to experience, understand, improve, and embrace life with autism. It chronicles the challenges and victories of each developmental stage from toddlerhood through young adulthood (including experiences with bullying, high school transitioning, college success, and employment). Inspiring hope and practical ideas, this book would be valuable for parents and professionals working with autistic individuals, or for anyone who wants to learn more about autism.

David and I hope that *See ME* is an enjoyable read as well as a memorable learning experience. Just as in David's classroom, he provides entertainment that teaches lessons!

Learn more at **www.petro-autism.com**

Thank you for sharing this resource with your children!

Sandy Petrovic

PART 1
The Story

Don't worry! You have begun this book. You just can't see me because I am invisible —or at least I feel that way.

Hi! I'm David and I am *autistic*. Another way to say it is that I am a person with *autism*.

Because of differences in how my brain works, I am different in how I feel, think, and act. I am different on the outside AND on the inside. Some of these differences you can see, and some you cannot. It is important to remember that each autistic person is unique from other autistic people! We do not look or act the same as each other even though we all have autism.

Are you curious about HOW I am different? Jump to "Part 2: My Autism" and read that section first!

Let me share with you a story about shedding my invisibility!

Because of my differences, some kids made fun of me while I was growing up. But worse for me was that most kids ignored me. I had the feeling that no one really knew me or cared about me. They left me out of their fun and acted like I was not even there. I felt invisible.

I had just started high school after moving to a new city. I didn't know many of the kids there. And after many weeks, I still ate lunch alone.

Every day, I would approach different kids sitting at different tables and ask, "Is this seat taken? Can I eat here?"

And they would answer, "No, we don't want you."
Or
"I'm saving that seat for someone."

Some kids didn't answer me at all. They just kept talking to each other and acted like I wasn't even there. Oh, I forgot! I was invisible to them.

After being turned away and not finding a seat, I would sadly take my lunch to the library and eat alone. I felt crushed once again. Lunch should be fun, but for me it was miserable.

Then one day, an amazing thing happened!

I was standing in the middle of the cafeteria looking for somewhere to sit YET AGAIN. One of the older, popular kids came up to ME, a young new kid, and said, "Hi! I'm Nick."

"I'm David."

"David, come sit at my table with my friends."

I was worried that once I met Nick's friends, they would turn me away like all the others. But to my great surprise, they welcomed me and asked me to have a seat!

I said, "Thank you!"

I walked over to their table feeling nervous and excited. This was what I had wanted for so long!

I was extremely eager to finally be part of a group! As I sat down, they started to have conversations with each other about what they did over the weekend. They talked about what was going on in each of their classes. And they talked about fun school events that were coming up. Even though I couldn't add anything to their conversations at that time, I still felt relief and pride that I was surrounded by a great group of teens.

I didn't even pay attention to what they were talking about. I just kept thinking, "Wow! I am actually sitting with a bunch of kids in the cafeteria! Not only did they not turn me away—they invited me!" And that is exactly what they did day after day for the rest of the school year.

The more I listened to this friendly group, the less *anxious* and more comfortable I felt. Lunch became something I looked forward to! I heard about all the fun they were having, and that got me thinking that maybe high school could be more good than bad.

After a while of me being a *listener*, my lunch buddies started to include me in their chats. They wanted to hear what I had to say, especially my thoughts and opinions. As my *confidence* grew, I took a chance to speak. And they listened to ME! They welcomed what I had to say. We started having conversations together.

The guys and girls at this table were all nice, bright, and creative students. Many of them were involved with the plays and pep rallies. I shared with them my desire to be an actor in the school's play, but that I had not been chosen. I expressed my disappointment and fear that I would never be considered for a part. It was the only activity that I tried out for. Without being in a play, I had nothing to do besides homework. I was good at acting, so I was confused about why I was rejected.

I didn't know what to do. They picked me back up and assured me that if I kept practicing and kept at it, I would find myself on a stage eventually. Not only were we talking, but we were also creating friendships!

I started to feel *SEEN.*

I realized that things would not change for the better unless I continued to try. I started to think about everything I wanted to *accomplish* during the rest of my time in high school. I became involved by rapping at the pep rallies, and I signed up to sing with music groups. But mostly, I kept working towards my biggest dream: performing in a musical.

I was no longer held back by fear. I started to realize that I might have to work a little harder to reach my goals, but that I could *achieve* them. And if I tried my best, no matter what the result, I would not wonder, "Could I have done more?"

I started off high school thinking that I would never end my losing streak. But after *persevering* and never giving up, I finally started to achieve success. And it spread from inside school to activities outside of school. In the end, I was involved in many plays and even gained a reputation for being a talented actor!

Just because I had special needs, it did not mean that I was stupid, as some kids had called me. I was actually very smart; I just learned in a different way. I realized that in order to do my best in school, I had to be taught in a way that worked best for me. So, I accepted *guidance* and the help of *tutors* that I had refused before. And as a result, my grades got WAY better!

I began to feel loved for who I was and how I was born. Before my lunch buddies, I felt sad, *hopeless*, and sometimes angry. I asked myself, "Why are people so nice to others and so mean to me? I did nothing, but they treat me like I am nothing."

After meeting Nick and the others, those *emotions* started to fade. I discovered new emotions like love, hope, and happiness. I wanted to pass these life-changing feelings on to others and make them feel loved too!

Other kids learned from watching Nick and started talking to me. Everything changed once I stopped trying to fit in and instead chose to stand out.

Once kids got to know me, they liked me and included me! I started to have more and more friends, and I **no longer felt invisible**!

Because Nick and his friends built me up, I started to see my WHOLE, true self.

I started to *discover* and *embrace* other things I liked about myself. I realized that I was not weird, like some kids called me. I was, and am, just different. I was NOT wrong or less *worthy*.

This is true for anyone who has any kind of a difference. Differences should be celebrated.

Nick saw the whole me when others didn't. His kindness made me feel visible and good about myself. He accepted me!

But I also had to put forth effort before I could feel more positive. I had to change my own thinking and accept my differences, too. **I had to see myself before others could see me!** I had to discover the good and special parts of me and believe, "Yes! I am OK just the way I am. I am good enough! I would make a good friend. I am different, but that does not make me wrong. I am cool in my own special way."

I enjoyed school so much after I was part of it! Realizing that Nick would soon be graduating, I took it upon myself to apply everything I learned. With my new *confidence*, I found the courage to start making new friends on my own!

I started to see my gifts and what I did well. Before, I did not see anything good about myself. But after a while, I learned that everyone in the world has strengths and *difficulties.*

> We are all good at different things, and no one is good at EVERYTHING. Sometimes we ALL need help.

When I was young, I just wanted to be like everyone else. But as I grew, I realized that everyone is different from every other person. On the other hand, we are all more the same than we are different! We all have similar wants, needs, dreams, and feelings. We all want to be loved and accepted for who we are.

Talk to me and get to know me for who I am on the inside! We should not make *assumptions.* I can be interesting and a great friend. And the same is true for everyone else!

I became proud of my differences AND of who I was deep down. I learned that I deserved the good things that happened. I was worthy of kindness, respect, and chances. I loved being me! And it all started with someone reaching out to me.

My message to you is, "Embrace a difference... and MAKE a difference!" Nick did that for me, and now I do that for others.

YOU have the same power to make a person feel seen, *recognized*, *appreciated*, and *worthwhile*.

The main rule is this: Treat others the way you would like to be treated. This is also known as the Golden Rule.

What about you?
What are your interesting differences?

You are beautiful. You matter.
You deserve all the good in this world.
And, just like me, you are seen!

"Embrace a difference...and MAKE a difference!"

PART 2
My Autism

Each autistic person is *unique* from other autistic people! We do not look or act the same as each other even though we all have autism.

For me, my thinking was stuck. I could not stray away from my way of doing things or my way of thinking about things. It was like my thoughts were placed in boxes in my brain and each thought couldn't mix or combine in any other way. I could not consider new ideas or different ways to do things. I was very rigid and couldn't grasp what others were thinking or wanted to do. I could only see things my way, and I wasn't very understanding of others. I had a hard time reorganizing the thoughts in my brain boxes.

I had many specific routines for how I did things. I ate the same foods for breakfast every day. For meals, I ate in a specific order. Even food groups needed to be eaten separately to enjoy and not confuse their flavors. I would eat the main course first and then the side dish; I would never take turns between them or mix up the foods.

It made me extremely uncomfortable if I had to stray from my way of doing things. If an activity was planned, my mind would be set on doing it. If the schedule changed, I had a tough time continuing with the rest of the day. An example would be if a substitute teacher showed up unexpectedly. It was terribly hard for me to handle change of any kind. It often looked like I was overreacting to things that should not have been a big deal.

I had an unusual way of playing with my toys. Instead of "playing" with them, I would organize them based on categories like size or color or how I saw them arranged on TV. For example, with "Snow White and the Seven Dwarfs," I would arrange the toy characters

David, age 6

to reenact the movie that was playing in my mind.

I had special interests that I always wanted to watch or do, like drawing. But wanting ONLY to draw and not wanting to stop became a problem for me. My interests occasionally changed, but they were usually different than other kids' interests. So, I mostly did them alone and away from the group.

I would research my topic to know everything about it and I would want to talk about it all the time. Eventually, I realized that not everyone WANTED to know every little detail that I learned. An example of this would be remembering **everything** about contestants on a reality show, such as "American Idol."

Another inside difference was in how I learned. Often, I needed things explained differently than others did before I could understand. I was smart, but sometimes I needed extra help and extra time to learn. It would take me longer to come up with answers to questions, but if people would wait, I **could** say what I thought. To balance that, my super memory was a great strength in helping me learn.

I also had a hard time making connections between thoughts or coming up with *original* ideas. One time, a teacher gave an assignment that required turning letters into animals. We were encouraged to use our imaginations. She drew an example on the board, and I just copied her example because I could not yet connect to my creative side, just like I could not yet make the connections needed to come to conclusions.

Over the years, with therapies and assistance, I did grow in all these skills. In fact, an autistic person's different thinking can often lead to amazingly creative ideas and new ways to do things! Some people with autism are brilliant experts in the fields of music and the arts, or in math, science, and computers.

My *senses* were sharper in some areas, but less in others. Bright lights, loud noises, some smells, and certain touches really bothered me, but other things I didn't seem to notice. For example, I couldn't tell how hot the water was in the shower and sometimes I forgot to eat because I couldn't feel myself getting hungry. Instead of growing in hunger, I would suddenly feel like I was starving. I loved tight hugs or touch made with great pressure, but I couldn't handle light brushes against my skin.

Haircuts were a nightmare. The hair falling on my skin felt like needles. Even walking barefoot on grass bothered me so much that I would have to jump back on the sidewalk after only a few tiptoes on it.

Most of my senses were magnified and the input from them was very extreme. In other words, I was *hypersensitive* in many areas. I had what I called my super sniffer. I would pick up smells that others with me didn't notice. The combined smells of the different kinds of food in the cafeteria would almost ruin my appetite when I walked in for lunch. Bright lights would bother me at first, especially if they were flashing, but then I usually got used to them.

The worst things for me were loud noises and buzzing sounds or sensations. Imagine all the places that were hard for me to go to! I loved playing basketball but watching it in person was tough. Squeaky shoes, the refs' whistles, coaches and fans yelling, and the scoreboard buzzing got to be too much. Sometimes I would take a break in the hall. But sometimes I just had to leave to get away from it all when my ear plugs were not blocking out enough noise. Some autistic kids wear noise-canceling headphones for this reason.

The same problems came with dances, carnivals, parties, and restaurants. Amusement parks were especially overwhelming. Adding on to what I just said, I experienced queasy feelings from the reckless and intense movements of the rides or from knocking into other people. I could only stay at all these places for a brief amount of time. I would get overwhelmed quickly with all the input, and I would get upset over things that others did not notice.

Some of my outside differences were easily seen by how I looked and acted. My walk had a unique style, and I had a tough time with *conversations*. I had a habit of getting into others' personal spaces by getting too close to them. I also spoke very loudly when I was little. I talked on and on about certain things that other kids were not interested in. I did not give others a chance to speak their minds. I wasn't clear on how to make friends, even though I wanted them. I had to learn these *social skills* that came easily to others.

Making human connections was also hard for other reasons. I understood the exact words that others said, but often not what they really meant. I couldn't tell if someone was joking or serious, and I didn't understand riddles, sarcasm, or puns. I couldn't recognize emotions on people's faces. I didn't even notice the clues in their gestures. A lot of times I missed out on what kids were actually saying.

I didn't often look into people's eyes while talking because it made me uncomfortable. I was able to concentrate more and absorb what they were saying better by NOT looking at them. Sometimes that made me seem like I wasn't paying attention, but I truly was listening the best way I could.

Some autistic kids spin in circles or move in unusual kinds of ways that feel good to them or calm them down. I always liked repeating sounds and phrases over and over again. I was copying the lines and voices from my favorite TV and movie characters. This "chit-chat," as my family called it, helped me to escape from stressful situations by helping me to cope. It was also my main source of entertainment when I was bored, and I enjoyed doing it.

You have just learned some of the main differences in me. They made me stand out from the other kids in my class. With the help of therapy and time, I made great advancements in my learning and coping skills. I learned the *accommodations* (help) that I needed, and still need, to be my best self. I will always be autistic, and I feel good about that. But back in the ninth grade, I struggled a lot!

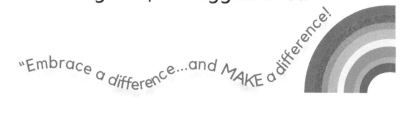

"Embrace a difference...and MAKE a difference!

PART 3
Activities
for You!

Your turn! Color this page!

Sketch art by Eeha Bhatt

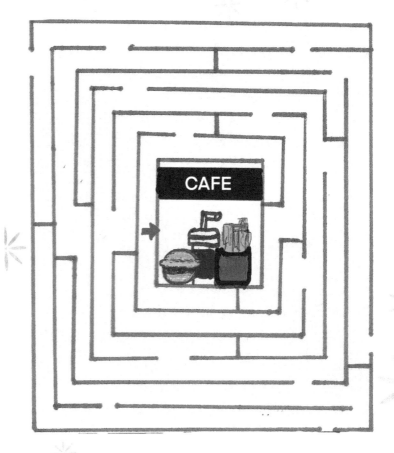

Find your way to a
lunch bunch who
will A-MAZE!

WORD SEARCH 1

Answer key in the back of the book.

N	I	H	O	V	I	K	L	W	W	N	H	B	V
A	S	S	U	M	P	T	I	O	N	S	Y	F	P
C	P	L	Q	H	N	L	Z	R	J	G	P	S	E
C	X	P	Y	J	T	S	H	T	Y	M	E	R	N
O	D	F	R	M	E	S	H	H	X	M	R	Q	M
M	E	I	X	E	E	X	D	Y	B	F	S	A	L
M	Z	T	E	R	C	Y	M	N	F	P	E	P	U
O	I	N	V	R	L	I	P	L	Q	W	N	X	C
D	N	K	M	T	H	H	A	M	Y	K	S	G	J
A	G	M	X	Z	X	N	X	T	U	S	I	S	B
T	O	N	B	N	I	G	K	X	E	K	T	E	X
I	C	K	Z	G	H	P	I	M	I	D	I	I	O
O	E	J	I	D	L	O	Y	P	B	T	V	T	V
N	R	R	Z	D	C	Y	E	A	K	R	E	L	G
S	O	J	B	C	E	Z	Y	L	T	P	A	U	Q
G	O	L	D	E	N	R	U	L	E	V	N	C	Z
E	L	I	H	W	H	T	R	O	W	Z	S	I	B
B	S	N	R	I	O	D	L	R	C	W	I	F	G
M	C	F	S	E	N	S	E	S	X	V	E	F	U
F	F	Z	P	M	N	Y	V	R	K	I	P	I	V
Y	P	R	G	B	K	K	L	D	L	S	V	D	G
U	N	P	E	R	S	E	V	E	R	I	N	G	H
O	C	R	F	A	W	T	Y	J	G	B	I	C	D
H	D	I	S	C	O	V	E	R	C	L	X	V	A
Z	O	G	P	E	R	Y	E	Z	Y	E	N	A	W

Embrace   Worthy   Visible   Persevering
Appreciated   Worthwhile   Golden Rule   Assumptions
Difficulties   Recognized   Original   Hypersensitive
Accommodations   Discover   Senses

WORD SEARCH 2

*Answer key in the back of the book.

K	I	U	M	I	Z	Q	J	Y	N	U	M	R	M
M	J	S	V	E	X	W	U	X	R	I	U	N	T
A	Q	M	Z	N	K	F	E	X	H	R	Q	J	J
C	C	L	E	T	X	C	M	A	E	E	D	L	R
C	B	O	U	B	W	D	O	N	Y	N	X	U	M
O	B	T	O	C	T	O	T	X	D	E	O	Q	M
M	C	W	X	I	R	Y	I	I	V	T	Q	Y	Y
P	C	R	O	T	U	T	O	O	B	S	L	Y	K
L	U	V	I	S	E	E	N	U	E	I	P	R	K
I	M	H	S	I	Z	C	S	S	F	L	F	J	D
S	N	O	I	T	A	S	R	E	V	N	O	C	T
H	Q	I	X	U	W	U	Y	E	E	S	Q	E	E
G	N	C	D	A	A	W	V	T	H	A	N	C	B
E	U	Q	I	N	U	R	N	V	R	H	U	N	J
Z	V	I	E	K	Q	T	B	R	E	G	A	E	U
G	P	E	D	L	T	F	I	E	V	T	U	D	N
L	N	U	I	A	L	W	R	S	J	X	Y	I	O
F	O	C	X	H	N	H	R	T	M	U	C	F	L
I	V	Z	R	C	C	C	Y	Q	H	S	C	N	R
C	N	C	W	O	S	A	E	M	R	I	V	O	V
A	S	S	E	L	E	P	O	H	N	B	H	C	R
B	Q	A	H	V	W	X	A	J	T	X	F	J	E
S	L	L	I	K	S	L	A	I	C	O	S	F	B
M	T	H	Y	R	B	O	P	T	A	T	P	F	B
U	D	U	R	A	T	U	G	T	K	M	F	J	A

Autistic	Guidance	Accomplish	Eager
Conversations	Autism	Tutor	Confidence
Anxious	Social Skills	Emotions	Achieve
Seen	Listener	Unique	Hopeless

CROSSWORD PUZZLE 1

*Answer key in the back of the book.

If you need more help, see the word search word banks.

Down

1. fulfill; get done
2. able to be seen
3. talking with someone
4. worried
7. guesses, unproven beliefs
9. longing to do something
10. no bright side; despair
11. complete; carry out
13. intense feelings and reactions

Across

1. having autism
5. feelings
6. help students learn
8. recognized; noticed for who you are
11. thankful for someone; valued
12. these are needed to communicate with others
14. someone special

CROSSWORD PUZZLE 2

*Answer key in the back of the book.

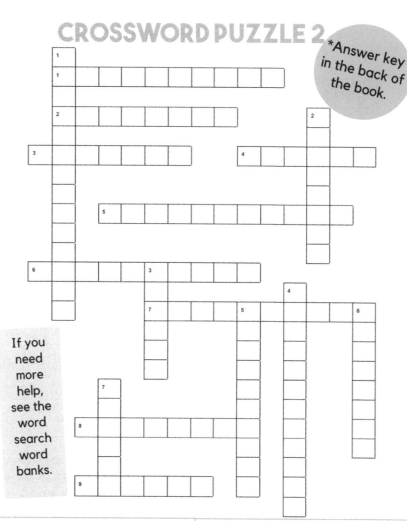

If you need more help, see the word search word banks.

Down
1. adjustments that help people succeed
2. counseling; coaching
3. deserving
4. struggles
5. act how you would want to be treated
6. to find
7. one and only; unlike others

Across
1. faith in yourself
2. first of its kind
3. accept; take in
4. a difference in development
5. to keep trying
6. valuable; of benefit
7. seen for who you are
8. hearing what someone says and means
9. allow information to be received from outside (e.g., sight, smell...)

TURN THIS "SAD LIB" INTO A "GLAD LIB"!!

Tony was walking around the playground feeling [**lonely**] because the other kids wouldn't [**speak to him**]. One day, a classmate came up to him and told him to [**get lost**]. Tony felt [**hopeless**] because all he ever wanted was to have just one friend to be there for him. [**Heartbroken**], Tony went off to [**cry**]. Tony was [**sad**] that things happened the way they did.

Tony was walking around the playground feeling _____ because the other kids wouldn't _____ . One day, a classmate came up to him and told him to _____. Tony felt _____ because all he ever wanted was to have just one friend to be there for him. _____, Tony went off to _____ . Tony was _____ that things happened the way they did.

Be kind to someone today!

"U"-NIQUE
Think about YOU!

What are 3 things you like about yourself?
1. _____
2. _____
3. _____

What are 3 things that make you different from other kids?
1. _____
2. _____
3. _____

What are 3 things that you are good at?
1. _____
2. _____
3. _____

What are 3 things you can do to brighten up someone's day?
1. _____
2. _____
3. _____

"U"-NIQUE
Think about YOU!

Draw your face as you see yourself.

Write a letter to one or two friends telling them how special they are!

Dear _____

_____
_____
_____
_____
_____
_____
_____
_____
_____
_____
_____
_____
_____
_____
_____
_____
_____
_____
_____
_____
_____
_____
_____

WORD SCRAMBLE

Unscramble these letters to spell *WORDS* that
were in Parts 1 and 2

ISNPEERREVG _____

CMOATDSCIOMOAN _____

UICGNAED _____

OTLWIWERHH _____

ISEDVORC _____

UIENUQ _____

MSTOSPINSUA _____

MAIUTS _____

IFIDTUSFLICE _____

ODUG RNELLE _____

MBCEERA _____

ESNSSE _____

Write a poem about kindness or worthiness
using the letters of "See Me"
at the beginning of each line.
See the next page for a sample.

S _____

E _____

E _____

M _____

E _____

SAMPLE POEM

Someone may call me worthless

Even though I'm not

Everyone's a flower, planted in a pot

My goals in life may be different than others', but

Everyone deserves to be loved as sisters and brothers

Reveal the hidden message by decoding the letters and characters

<table>
<tr><td>1 – A</td><td>7 – G</td><td>13 – M</td><td>19 – S</td><td>25 – Y</td></tr>
<tr><td>2 – B</td><td>8 – H</td><td>14 – N</td><td>20 – T</td><td>26 – Z</td></tr>
<tr><td>3 – C</td><td>9 – I</td><td>15 – O</td><td>21 – U</td><td>27 – ,</td></tr>
<tr><td>4 – D</td><td>10 – J</td><td>16 – P</td><td>22 – V</td><td>28 – .</td></tr>
<tr><td>5 – E</td><td>11 – K</td><td>17 – Q</td><td>23 – W</td><td>29 – !</td></tr>
<tr><td>6 – F</td><td>12 – L</td><td>18 – R</td><td>24 – X</td><td>30 – ?</td></tr>
</table>

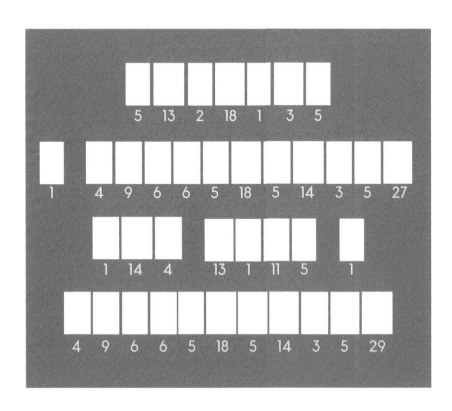

5 13 2 18 1 3 5

1   4 9 6 6 5 18 5 14 3 5 27

1 14 4   13 1 11 5   1

4 9 6 6 5 18 5 14 3 5 29

CONNECT THE DOTS

Connect the dots to see a gesture that can lift someone up.

Find these hidden foods:

BANANA
PIZZA
COOKIE
STRAWBERRY

Think Time!

Did you notice on the cover that the "E" in the "ME" of the title is backwards?

Why do you think that is?
What could the "E" facing backwards mean?

_____
_____
_____
_____
_____
_____
_____
_____

David's Thoughts:

It is OK to be different! Being different does not mean that you are wrong or not as important as others. My "E" proudly faces another direction. The backwards "E" represents my comfort and openness to being different—and owning it! I know that with my differences, I can "make" a difference by helping others realize the truth and beauty in diversity (variety). Importantly, as people tried to get to know and understand me, my backwards E started to be recognized as interesting and unique in a positive way!

Answer Key

WORD SEARCH 1 KEY

R	E	Y	Y	E	R	U	M	W	W	D	H	J	L
A	S	S	U	M	P	T	I	O	N	S	Y	R	B
C	P	E	X	M	C	N	P	R	D	C	P	L	I
C	Z	P	E	V	P	A	M	T	T	F	E	F	V
O	D	A	R	K	W	K	O	H	Z	H	R	A	M
M	E	J	T	E	G	Z	H	Y	G	Z	S	B	R
M	Z	J	R	J	C	Y	R	W	V	D	E	S	E
O	I	H	R	H	Q	I	D	L	A	C	N	M	J
D	N	J	A	T	T	X	A	D	E	H	S	F	D
A	G	I	A	K	E	N	I	T	M	O	I	S	Z
T	O	M	J	H	I	F	N	P	E	N	T	E	R
I	C	W	I	G	G	H	P	U	M	D	I	I	G
O	E	U	I	Q	N	M	C	X	B	E	V	T	I
N	R	R	H	B	G	I	Z	Y	T	D	E	L	Y
S	O	U	A	L	W	W	R	O	E	D	A	U	M
G	O	L	D	E	N	R	U	L	E	R	O	C	K
E	L	I	H	W	H	T	R	O	W	A	U	I	O
X	L	C	I	F	U	T	E	Q	X	O	Q	F	Z
I	I	Q	S	E	N	S	E	S	L	V	E	F	U
U	R	X	Q	M	G	G	J	V	D	I	P	I	Z
P	Z	D	F	B	X	G	E	Q	F	S	Z	D	R
Y	X	P	E	R	S	E	V	E	R	I	N	G	Q
R	R	V	O	A	K	Y	O	Q	F	B	L	W	R
N	D	I	S	C	O	V	E	R	J	L	R	G	N
G	K	S	L	E	Q	U	D	V	O	E	I	L	F

WORD SEARCH 2 KEY

C	B	R	I	R	T	R	T	B	V	O	G	W	I
H	W	L	J	E	F	W	B	J	R	U	A	Z	B
A	Y	X	A	W	G	W	E	Q	S	R	I	P	Z
C	B	H	P	M	N	I	M	A	X	E	W	J	J
C	T	X	V	W	K	A	O	N	D	N	W	A	O
O	E	G	R	C	O	O	T	X	X	E	S	J	B
M	Y	S	Z	I	M	N	I	I	L	T	K	V	J
P	D	R	O	T	U	T	O	O	W	S	O	J	G
L	M	J	M	S	E	E	N	U	L	I	R	B	J
I	N	J	A	I	L	H	S	S	M	L	G	T	H
S	N	O	I	T	A	S	R	E	V	N	O	C	N
H	U	L	N	U	G	M	N	C	G	E	F	E	P
G	N	C	D	A	A	Y	R	G	W	Z	H	C	Z
E	U	Q	I	N	U	E	X	Y	A	A	P	N	H
X	V	I	T	X	B	T	E	R	E	G	A	E	M
C	P	E	D	B	E	Y	I	I	G	J	K	D	R
W	V	O	I	A	K	S	V	H	N	A	I	G
M	R	K	R	H	N	I	X	G	M	N	Z	F	I
H	E	B	I	L	C	C	O	A	E	T	Z	N	T
Y	N	U	J	M	Y	A	E	Z	O	K	I	O	M
S	S	S	E	L	E	P	O	H	M	B	Y	C	H
H	P	W	G	J	V	S	P	A	A	N	Z	K	A
S	L	L	I	K	S	L	A	I	C	O	S	N	S
B	K	I	H	X	O	N	N	K	D	V	G	V	R
M	T	V	Y	W	Z	H	U	J	C	K	L	V	U

CROSSWORD PUZZLE 1

Across / Down grid entries:

- ¹AUTISTIC
- ²VISIBLE
- ³CONVERSATION
- ⁴ANXIOUS
- ⁵EMOTIONS
- ⁶TUTOR
- ⁷ASSUMPTIONS
- ⁸SEEN
- ⁹EAGER
- ¹⁰HOPLESS
- ¹¹APPRECIATED
- ¹²SOCIALSKILLS
- ¹³HYPERSENSITIVE
- ¹⁴ME

CROSSWORD PUZZLE 2

Across:
1. CONFIDENCE
2. ORIGINAL
3. EMBRACE
4. AUTISM
5. PERSEVERING
6. WORTHWHILE
7. RECOGNIZE
8. LISTENER
9. SENSES

Down:
1. ACCOMMODATIONS
2. GUIDANCE
3. WHOLE
4. DIFFICULTIES
5. GOLDENRULE
6. DISCOVER
7. UNIQUE

WORD SCRAMBLE KEY

ISNPEERREVG ————————→ **PERSEVERING**

CMOATDSCIOMOAN ——→ **ACCOMMODATIONS**

UICGNAED ——————————→ **GUIDANCE**

OTLWIWERHH ——————→ **WORTHWHILE**

ISEDVORC ——————————→ **DISCOVER**

UIENUQ ————————————→ **UNIQUE**

MSTOSPINSUA ——————→ **ASSUMPTIONS**

MAIUTS ——————————————→ **AUTISM**

IFIDTUSFLICE ——————→ **DIFFICULTIES**

ODUG RNELLE ——————→ **GOLDEN RULE**

MBCEERA ——————————→ **EMBRACE**

ESNSSE ——————————————→ **SENSES**

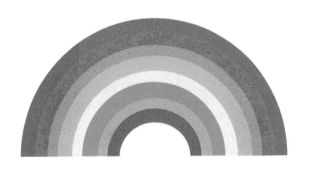

About the Author

David Petrovic is an autistic middle school teacher who graduated from Notre Dame College in South Euclid, Ohio. He received a master's degree in theology from St. Joseph's College in Maine. Besides being a teacher and author, David is also a national speaker who most enjoys presenting to youth and teen audiences. Bullied in the past, David's greatest passion lies in sharing his messages of kindness, hope, and never giving up.

Other books by David Petrovic and Sandy Petrovic:
Expect a Miracle: Understanding and Living with Autism
(Revised 2nd Edition)

One chapter (pages 180-195) in:
Life After Lockdown: Resetting Perceptions of Autism

www.petro-autism.com

Available on Amazon

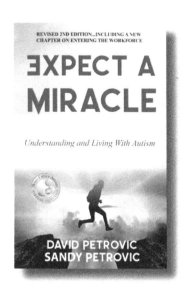

This 2-time award-winning book enables readers to experience, understand, improve, and embrace life with autism, whether personally or professionally.

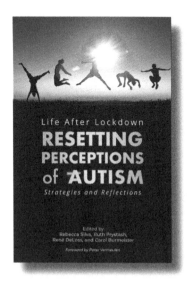

This book provides practical advice but also addresses the deeper issues of respect, dignity, and the importance of providing everyone with the opportunity to build a meaningful life.

Chapter contribution by David and Sandy.

Made in the USA
Columbia, SC
23 September 2022

67340273R00046